ANXIETY AND FEAR IN DAILY LIFE

CHILDHOOD FEARS AND ANXIETIES

Anxiety and Fear in Daily Life

Catastrophes

Crime and Terrorism

Family Fears

Medical Fears

Nighttime Fears

Phobias

School Fears

Separation Anxiety

Social Fears

Symptoms and Treatments of
Anxiety Disorders

CHILDHOOD FEARS
AND ANXIETIES

ANXIETY AND FEAR IN DAILY LIFE

H.W. POOLE

SERIES CONSULTANT
ANNE S. WALTERS, Ph.D.

Emma Pendleton Bradley Hospital

Warren Alpert Medical School of
Brown University

MASON CREST

Mason Crest
450 Parkway Drive, Suite D
Broomall, PA 19008
www.masoncrest.com

© 2018 by Mason Crest, an imprint of National Highlights, Inc. All rights reserved. No part of this publication may be reproduced or transmitted in any form or by any means, electronic or mechanical, including photocopying, recording, taping, or any information storage and retrieval system, without permission from the publisher.

MTM Publishing, Inc.
435 West 23rd Street, #8C
New York, NY 10011
www.mtmpublishing.com

President: Valerie Tomaselli
Vice President, Book Development: Hilary Poole
Designer: Annemarie Redmond
Copyeditor: Peter Jaskowiak
Editorial Assistant: Leigh Eron

Series ISBN: 978-1-4222-3721-2
Hardback ISBN: 978-1-4222-3722-9
E-Book ISBN: 978-1-4222-8055-3

Library of Congress Cataloging-in-Publication Data
Names: Poole, Hilary W., author.
Title: Anxiety and fear in daily life / by H.W. Poole; Series Consultant:
   Anne S. Walters, Ph.D.
Description: Broomall, PA: Mason Crest, [2018] | Series: Childhood fears and
   anxieties | Includes index.
Identifiers: LCCN 2017003479 (print) | LCCN 2017020869 (ebook) | ISBN
   9781422280553 (ebook) | ISBN 9781422237229 (hardback: alk. paper)
Subjects: LCSH: Anxiety in children—Juvenile literature. | Anxiety—Juvenile
   literature.
Classification: LCC BF723.A5 (ebook) | LCC BF723.A5 P66 2018 (print) | DDC
   152.4/6—dc23
LC record available at https://lccn.loc.gov/2017003479.

Printed and bound in the United States of America.

First printing
9 8 7 6 5 4 3 2 1

QR CODES AND LINKS TO THIRD PARTY CONTENT
You may gain access to certain third party content ("Third Party Sites") by scanning and using the QR Codes that appear in this publication (the "QR Codes"). We do not operate or control in any respect any information, products or services on such Third Party Sites linked to by us via the QR Codes included in this publication and we assume no responsibility for any materials you may access using the QR Codes. Your use of the QR Codes may be subject to terms, limitations, or restrictions set forth in the applicable terms of use or otherwise established by the owners of the Third Party Sites. Our linking to such Third Party Sites via the QR Codes does not imply an endorsement or sponsorship of such Third Party Sites, or the information, products or services offered on or through the Third Party Sites, nor does it imply an endorsement or sponsorship of this publication by the owners of such Third Party Sites.

TABLE OF CONTENTS

Series Introduction 6

Chapter One: What Is Fear? 9

Chapter Two: Fear and Growing Up 19

Chapter Three: Anxiety Troubles 27

Chapter Four: Taking Charge of Anxiety 37

Further Reading 44

Series Glossary 45

Index 47

About the Advisor 48

About the Author 48

Photo Credits 48

Key Icons to Look for:

Words to Understand: These words with their easy-to-understand definitions will increase the reader's understanding of the text, while building vocabulary skills.

Sidebars: This boxed material within the main text allows readers to build knowledge, gain insights, explore possibilities, and broaden their perspectives by weaving together additional information to provide realistic and holistic perspectives.

Educational Videos: Readers can view videos by scanning our QR codes, which will provide them with additional educational content to supplement the text. Examples include news coverage, moments in history, speeches, iconic sports moments, and much more.

Text-Dependent Questions: These questions send the reader back to the text for more careful attention to the evidence presented there.

Research Projects: Readers are pointed toward areas of further inquiry connected to each chapter. Suggestions are provided for projects that encourage deeper research and analysis.

Series Glossary of Key Terms: This back-of-the-book glossary contains terminology used throughout the series. Words found here increase the reader's ability to read and comprehend higher-level books and articles in this field.

SERIES INTRODUCTION

Who among us does not have memories of an intense childhood fear? Fears and anxieties are a part of *every* childhood. Indeed, these fears are fodder for urban legends and campfire tales alike. And while the details of these legends and tales change over time, they generally have at their base predictable childhood terrors such as darkness, separation from caretakers, or bodily injury.

We know that fear has an evolutionary component. Infants are helpless, and, compared to other mammals, humans have a very long developmental period. Fear ensures that curious children will stay close to caretakers, making them less likely to be exposed to danger. This means that childhood fears are adaptive, making us more likely to survive, and even thrive, as a species.

Unfortunately, there comes a point when fear and anxiety cease to be useful. This is especially problematic today, for there has been a startling increase in anxiety among children and adolescents. In fact, 25 percent of 13- to 18-year-olds now have mild to moderate anxiety, and the *median* age of onset for anxiety disorders is just 11 years old.

Why might this be? Some say that the contemporary United States is a nation preoccupied with risk, and it is certainly possible that our children are absorbing this preoccupation as well. Certainly, our exposure to potential threats has never been greater. We see graphic images via the media and have more immediate news of all forms of disaster. This can lead our children to feel more vulnerable, and it may increase the likelihood that they respond with fear. If children based their fear on the news that they see on Facebook or on TV, they would dramatically overestimate the likelihood of terrible things happening.

As parents or teachers, what do we do about fear? As in other areas of life, we provide our children with guidance and education on a daily basis. We teach them about the signs and feelings of fear. We discuss and normalize typical fear reactions, and support them in tackling difficult situations despite fear. We explain—and demonstrate by example—how to identify "negative thinking traps" and generate positive coping thoughts instead.

But to do so effectively, we might need to challenge some of our own assumptions about fear. Adults often assume that they must protect their children from fear and help them to avoid scary situations, when sometimes the best course is for the child to face the fear and conquer it. This is counterintuitive for many adults: after all, isn't it our job to reassure our children and help them feel better? Yes, of course! Except when it isn't. Sometimes they need us to help them confront their fears and move forward anyway.

That's where these volumes come in. When it comes to fear, balanced information is critical. Learning about fear as it relates to many different areas can help us to help our children remember that although you don't choose whether to be afraid, you do choose how to handle it. These volumes explore the world of childhood fears, seeking to answer important questions: How much is too much? And how can fear be positive, functioning to mobilize us in the face of danger?

Fear gives us the opportunity to step up and respond with courage and resilience. It pushes us to expand our sphere of functioning to areas that might feel unfamiliar or risky. When we are a little nervous or afraid, we tend to prepare a little more, look for more information, ask more questions—and all of this can function to help us expand the boundaries of our lives in a positive direction. So, while fear might *feel* unpleasant, there is no doubt that it can have a positive outcome.

Let's teach our children that.

—Anne Walters, Ph.D.
Chief Psychologist, Emma Pendleton Bradley Hospital
Clinical Associate Professor,
Alpert Medical School of Brown University

Fear helped keep our ancient ancestors safe from predators.

CHAPTER ONE

WHAT IS FEAR?

Let's imagine we can travel back in time, to about 200,000 years ago. It is the dawn of our ancestors— the *Homo sapiens*. And let's picture two individuals. To tell them apart, we'll nickname one Grr and the other Eek. Grr has a quick temper; he acts first and thinks later (if at all). Eek is more timid; sometimes he can't sleep because he keeps thinking about the many threats that exist outside his cave.

One day, a lion comes prowling around. Grr does not want a lion near the cave; it makes him feel threatened. So he jumps up, grabs a big rock, and goes outside to bash the lion on the head. Meanwhile, Eek stays inside. He also feels threatened, but the feeling causes him to hang back instead of acting. As a matter of fact, Eek had recently been worrying that a lion might show up. That worry caused him to save some extra food. He figures he'll wait in the cave until the lion gets bored and wanders away.

What are the likely outcomes for Grr and Eek?

We don't know for sure what will happen. It's possible that Grr will succeed in killing the lion. If

WORDS TO UNDERSTAND

adaptive: helpful behavior that enables people to improve their situation.

adrenaline: a substance created by the body in times of stress or excitement.

amygdala: part of the brain that is involved in instinct and emotion.

maladaptive: unhelpful behavior that makes a situation worse.

outcomes: results.

perception: awareness; what we see or understand.

If feeling worried inspires us to act—for example, studying before a hard test—then it's useful, but...

so, Grr's community will have a feast, and he will be considered a hero. Unfortunately, the more likely outcome is that the lion will win. If so, Grr will not be around very long. So, we can say that a *likely* short-term outcome is Grr's death, and a likely long-term outcome is that he won't have any children. Grr's hot temper will probably disappear along with the rest of him.

As for Eek, it's possible that his food-saving plan will fail. Maybe the lion *won't* get bored—maybe it will lurk outside for days while Eek slowly starves. But the more likely outcome is that lion *will* get hungry and wander off to hunt something else. In that case, a short-term outcome is Eek's survival, and a long-term outcome is the creation of lots of little Eeks to carry on the family tradition of lion avoidance.

Rash people like Grr still exist, of course! But, in general, humans tend to be more like Eek. As a species, we evolved to worry. And that's not a bad thing. The ability to imagine outcomes and make plans is a major reason why humans were able to advance from those caves of Grr and Eek's day.

However, sometimes worrying can go too far. Let's picture Eek again. He did a good job staying out of the way of that lion. His worry caused him to make a plan (saving food) that saved his life. But there's a catch. Once the lion has left, it's important

...if it just makes us upset for no real reason, then worry can be a problem.

that Eek then go outside and return to whatever he was doing. If Eek becomes *so* worried that he decides to *never* leave the cave, then he has a big problem. Sure, it might be safer to never leave the cave, but then Eek can't find more food. He also won't meet the future mother of all those little Eeks. The point is, Eek's worry is useful, but only to a point. Eventually, he has to recover from his fear and get on with his life.

How much fear is too much? What if Eek *knows* that it's time to stop worrying, but he can't seem to do it? What does he do then? In this book, we will try to find some answers to these questions.

FEAR: WHAT'S IT GOOD FOR?

The feeling of fear is the human body's response to a threat. It begins in a part of the brain called the amygdala. The amygdala has a few different jobs, but the most important has to do with the perception of danger. When the brain detects a threat, the amygdala sounds a chemical "alarm" in the body. The body begins producing more adrenaline, which causes the heart to beat faster and breathing to increase. Blood rushes to the muscles. Senses such as sight and hearing become heightened, while the body's sensitivity to pain decreases. These reactions are often described as a "fight-or-flight" response (see box on page 14).

EDUCATIONAL VIDEO

Check out this video about the difference between anxiety and fear.

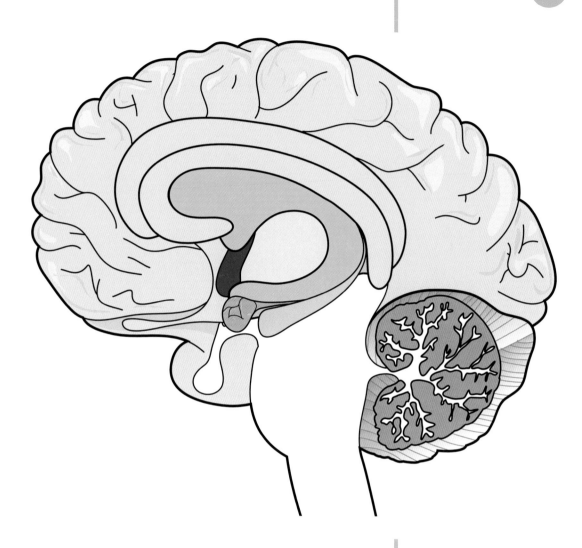

These physical effects can make the experience of fear very unpleasant. You feel tense, you start sweating, your stomach feels upset. Not fun. But at the same time, the physical effects of fear are also making you more aware of your surroundings than you would normally be. This means you are better prepared to respond to whatever happens next. The surge of adrenaline enables humans to do things

The human brain in cross-section. The amygdala is the rounded orange bit; you have one on each side of the brain.

THE THREE F'S

When our primitive men, Grr and Eek, heard a lion outside their cave, they had a decision to make. Do they attack the lion or avoid it? This is the same decision every person makes when faced with a threat. This dilemma even has its own name: the fight-or-flight response.

Humans today don't have to struggle for survival nearly as much as we did thousands of years ago. But our fight-or-flight response still exists. Even if you're afraid of a loud sound in the dark or of sitting down for a hard test at school, you will still experience that same fight-or-flight response that Grr and Eek did.

Although the choice is usually expressed as "fight" or "flight," there is also a third option, called "freeze." Animals often choose freeze as a response to predators—they simply stay very still and hope the predator won't notice them. The way deer stop in front of oncoming cars is a famous case of freezing in the face of a threat—that's where we get the expression "caught like a deer in headlights."

Humans also sometimes freeze in response to danger. This is why it's usually unfair to criticize a crime victim for not fighting back. We might want to fight, but sometimes fear makes us unable to do so.

Deer really do tend to freeze when confronted with an oncoming car.

they couldn't otherwise—fight harder, think faster, run farther, and so on.

This is why fear is often called an "adaptive response." The word *adaptive* refers to the fact that fear helps us respond to our circumstances in useful ways. However, too much fear can be *maladaptive*— that's the term for behavior that is unhelpful. For instance, if Eek becomes so afraid of lions that he never leaves his cave, that's a maladaptive response.

FEAR VERSUS ANXIETY

Fear is an extreme emotion. We all experience it from time to time, but hopefully we don't feel truly afraid very often. What we do experience often is the nasty little brother of fear, known as anxiety. Anxiety and fear are pretty similar, but there is one huge difference between them.

Let's imagine that you walk past a neighbor's house, and his angry dog chases you. When you look at the dog's sharp teeth and hear its angry bark, what you are feeling in that moment is fear. The dog is right there, and he will bite you if he can.

The next day, you walk past that neighbor's house again. You will probably feel some of that same emotion. Your pulse races, your breathing speeds up, and you get ready to run.

Here's the difference: there's no dog.

But it doesn't matter, because your brain is doing all the work. You are remembering the scary dog

Some fears are learned; if you know your neighbor has an angry guard dog, you might be wary of it whenever you pass by.

from last time, and you are concerned that he will come back. So you feel all the same symptoms as before, but there actually is no threat. You're no longer responding to the *threat* of the dog; you are responding to the *idea* of the dog. That's anxiety.

Fear is a response to an actual threat right in front of you. Anxiety is a response to past and potential threats. In other words, anxiety is a response to things that *might* happen. Here's another example: if your teacher gives a pop quiz and you don't know any of the answers, that feeling in the pit of your stomach is fear. But if you wake up every morning feeling scared because there *might* be a pop quiz—even though you have no idea if that will actually happen—that's anxiety.

You may be thinking, "Wow, anxiety is pointless and terrible." And yeah, in some cases, that's true. But, it's important to understand that anxiety can be helpful, too. Remember Eek? He worried about that lion long before the lion showed up. Worry caused him to make a plan, and that plan saved his life. If you feel anxious about a pop quiz, you may study harder. That would be a way of putting anxiety to good use. When anxiety inspires people to action, it can be very helpful.

The problem is, anxiety often doesn't inspire us. More often, it freaks us out, ruins our sleep, and even makes us sick. In the next chapter, we're going to look at some of the anxieties and fears that are a typical part of growing up. Then we'll look at how anxiety can get out of control and what we can do about it.

RESEARCH PROJECT

Make two lists, one titled "Fears" and the other "Anxieties." Think about moments in your life when you feel afraid—were your feelings caused by real threats (fear) or possible ones (anxiety)? If you can, talk to some adults about their fears and anxieties, and add those to your list. Which list is longer? Why do you think that is?

TEXT-DEPENDENT QUESTIONS

1. What is the difference between an adaptive and a maladaptive response?

2. What part of the brain registers fear?

3. What's the difference between fear and anxiety?

Noises that are no big deal during the day can seem scary at night.

CHAPTER TWO

FEAR AND GROWING UP

Fear and anxiety are both caused by our perception of danger. Sometimes the danger is real, such as the angry dog discussed in chapter one, and sometimes it isn't, such as our memory of the angry dog. The interesting thing is, our bodies react in roughly the same way, regardless of whether the danger is real or not.

One thing that does vary a lot is what exactly people perceive as dangerous. Everybody is different; one person can look at a situation and see all kinds of possible threats, while someone else might view the same situation as no threat at all. Some of this is just a matter of personality. Certain people are just more fearful than others. Remember our cavemen, Grr and Eek? They responded to the same threat in totally different ways. Different people might fear different things, or they might react differently to those fears.

In addition to personality, another factor can be age. As we grow, our understanding of the world changes. And as our perceptions change, our fears

WORDS TO UNDERSTAND

attachment: strong affection for someone or something.

object permanence: the concept that people and things continue to exist when we don't see them.

probability: the likelihood that an event might happen.

wary: very cautious or suspicious.

COMMON KID FEARS BY AGE

- Birth to age 2: strangers, separation anxiety, loud noises, mascots.
- Age 2 to 6: darkness, dogs, monsters, or other imaginary things.
- Age 6 to 13: doctors, natural disasters, pain or injury, loss of parents.

change as well. Babies tend to fear certain things, while young kids tend to fear other things, and older kids still others. This chapter will look at fears that tend to be common among people at different stages of life. (By the way: sometimes people call these "normal" fears, but we are going to stay away from the word *normal* here. You may have more fears than we list here, or fewer, or different fears entirely—that doesn't make you not normal.)

STRANGER DANGER

If you've spent any time around babies, you've probably noticed how helpless they are. They can't talk, feed themselves, or even move around much at first. It takes time for babies to learn basic skills. So it makes sense that their fears tend to be pretty basic as well.

Many babies don't like unfamiliar things. They might be upset by a big change in their house, for example. A lot of babies are easily scared by loud noises. Specific fears can vary a lot: some babies are happy to held by adults they don't know, but they might fear the family dog. Other babies love animals, but strangers make them **wary**.

As babies grow, their awareness of the world increases. For example, they may notice when a person leaves a room, but they may not be sure the person will come back. The question becomes, "If I can't see something, does it still exist?" *You* know that of course it does—if your mom leaves the room, she doesn't disappear forever. But babies aren't always so sure, and this can be frightening.

In fact, this fear is so common that it even has its own name: *separation anxiety.* Separation anxiety is common among very young children (around one to two years of age). This is when children develop strong attachments to their parents. They understand that their parents are different from all other people in the world. And the idea that their parents could go away is very frightening. Almost all children go

Some little kids are just naturally more anxious than others.

OBJECT PERMANENCE

Babies enter this world with a whole lot to learn. A lot of things that seem obvious to you are new and fascinating to a baby. For instance, if you are at school right now, does your bedroom still exist? Well, yeah, obviously . . . unless you're a baby. That's because babies don't understand the concept of object permanence.

Object permanence describes the very simple idea that objects don't disappear just because you can't see them. Did you ever wonder why babies find peek-a-boo so funny? It's because hiding and then revealing your face is a way of playing with the idea of object permanence. To a baby, this is a delightful experience. In fact, some have described peek-a-boo as the first "joke" that babies learn: *I can't see your face—does it still exist? Yes, yes it does!*

But this is also why babies are so easily frightened. They might be thinking, "Mom just left. . . . Oh no, is she gone forever?!" It usually takes between about eight months to one year before babies truly understand that objects don't disappear. And it takes even longer for them to accept that Mom can leave the room *and* come back later.

The game of peek-a-boo plays with babies' understanding of object permanence.

through this phase at least briefly. (For more on this topic, see the volume *Separation Anxiety* in this set.)

Very young children may also be afraid of dogs and any other animals (or even other children) who don't behave in predictable ways. Again, this is a common part of development, and again, it was adaptive for our ancestors. If we think about Eek's children, for example, the more fearful they were of strange animals, the less likely they were to get eaten. Another common fear for very young children is the fear of heights. Guess when that usually develops? Yep, it crops up right around the same time most children are learning how to walk.

Even the fear of vegetables, which parents find so frustrating, is probably adaptive. Being suspicious of new foods would have been a good trait in Eek's children, because it would have kept them from eating things that might be poisonous.

Overall, most young children don't like surprises very much. Repetition can be very comforting at this age, and new things can be scary. This is why so many young children love to hear the same stories over and over.

THINGS THAT GO BUMP

As babies turn into little kids, they start to realize that there's a lot they don't understand. But they are still young enough that they aren't sure what is real and what isn't. These two factors can be a scary combination! This is an age where nightmares can be

EDUCATIONAL VIDEO

Check out this video for little kids who have separation anxiety. Would it have helped you at that age?

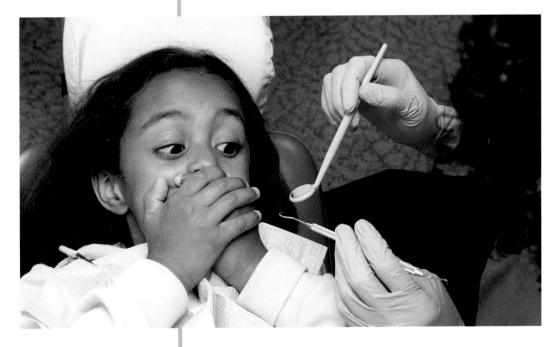

As we get older, our anxieties shift from imaginary things to real things.

at their scariest—it's hard for younger kids to tell the difference between fantasy and reality. Kids between two and four years of age are often afraid of the dark. They may imagine that there is a monster under the bed or in the closet.

As we get older, we get better at telling the difference between what's real and what isn't. By the time kids start school, most of them have outgrown their fear of monsters. Unfortunately, those imaginary fears are replaced by fears of events that are all too real. Going to the dentist can be scary, for example. So can getting a shot at the doctor's office. Some kids worry that something bad could happen to their parents, or they worry about a fire in their house. Scary news stories on TV might make some kids afraid of a burglar, a hurricane, or a terrorist attack.

WILD WORLD

Although school-age kids are sophisticated enough to know that monsters don't exist, they might still need to improve their understanding of probability. Probability has to do with how likely it is that a particular event will happen. Let's take terrorism, for instance. Unlike monsters, terrorists do exist. Therefore, being afraid of a terrorist attack is more realistic than being afraid of a monster.

But the interesting thing is, it's not *much* more realistic. The probability of someone being killed by a terrorist is 1 in 20 million. For comparison, the likelihood of someone being killed in a car crash is 1 in 19,000. On your list of worries, terrorists should actually rate quite low. Don't feel bad if that's not the case, though—even adults are not very good at figuring out the difference between a real threat and an imaginary one.

RESEARCH PROJECT

Interview people of different ages (friends, family members, and so on) about what they were afraid of when they were younger. Ask what made them scared and at what age? Keep a running list of the answers and then analyze what you've found. What are the most common fears? Why do you think that is?

TEXT-DEPENDENT QUESTIONS

1. What are some typical fears of babies?

2. What is object permanence?

3. How does the concept of probability relate to anxiety?

Insomnia is a common reaction to anxiety.

CHAPTER THREE

ANXIETY TROUBLES

If you have a physical illness like the flu, there are certain symptoms that you can expect. You'll probably have a runny nose, your throat might be sore, and you'll probably spend time curled up in bed. The flu virus inside you causes particular effects on your body and on how you act. And these effects are pretty hard to miss! Pretty much anybody will be able to tell, just by looking at you, that you are ill.

Anxiety doesn't always work like that. In some extreme cases, it might be obvious that someone has a problem. Someone may be so anxious that she is afraid to go outside at all, for example. But in daily life, it's not always clear whether anxiety is "typical" or a problem. This chapter explains some particular signals that might suggest a problem with anxiety.

But it is important to remember that everybody is different. Not everybody who struggles with

WORDS TO UNDERSTAND

hormones: substances that regulate bodily functions.

insomnia: an ongoing condition of not being able to fall asleep or stay asleep for long.

reassurance: a promise that everything is going to be okay.

anxiety will have the same experience. Also, just because something in this chapter might remind you of yourself, that *does not automatically* mean that you have a problem with anxiety. However, understanding these effects may help you better understand what is going on, either in yourself or in the mind of someone else.

PHYSICAL SIGNS OF ANXIETY

Butterflies in your stomach. Heart thumping in your chest. Dry mouth, weak knees. You've

Waiting outside the principal's office can definitely bring on anxiety symptoms.

probably experienced these sensations at some point—maybe it was right before you had to give a presentation in class, or maybe it was the last time you were sitting outside the principal's office. Those physical symptoms are sometimes called *stress reactions.* They are ways that the body responds to a perceived threat.

When the brain perceives a threat, it releases a substance called adrenaline. It's the adrenaline that's causing your heart to beat faster. Blood is being sent quickly all around the body, in order to make you ready to face whatever is coming. This can be extremely useful—stress reactions can make us more focused and more ready to respond to whatever happens next. Adrenaline also increases physical strength and agility for short periods. Unfortunately, a side-effect of the adrenaline (plus other hormones that are also released when a person is under stress) is that sick feeling in your stomach.

Normally, these physical symptoms go away as soon as the "threat" has passed. The problem for people with anxiety disorders is that although the threats feel very real, they actually aren't. This makes it much harder for them to "get over" those physical symptoms. For instance, if someone has *cynophobia* (a severe fear of dogs), just seeing a photo of a dog could cause a powerful physical reaction. It doesn't help to know that it's not a real dog and that there's no danger. The body has the same stress reaction anyway.

Anxiety can cause insomnia, too. People with anxiety can often be restless and have trouble concentrating—that's due to the anxiety nagging at them, distracting them from whatever they'd rather be doing. Again, this is because that stress reaction won't shut off the way it is supposed to.

SEEKING REASSURANCE

One sign that someone might be struggling with anxiety is if he or she needs reassurance constantly. Anxious kids want to be told that "everything will be okay." They ask a lot of questions, like, "Is the front door really locked?" or "Will we really be on time for school?" and so on. And they tend to ask those same questions over and over again. Doctors even have a term for this: *reassurance-seeking behavior.* The problem is, the reassurance doesn't last for very long. If someone is struggling with anxiety, no amount of reassurance will ever be enough.

Let's imagine a girl who is worried that her dad will get in a car accident on the way home from work. She asks her mom for reassurance that Dad will get home safely. Her mom says, "Of course he will, honey; your dad is an excellent driver!" The girl thinks, "Good point!" That answer makes her feel better for a little while.

Opposite: Parents can offer a lot of comfort, but ultimately, some anxieties just have to be faced.

But before long, the worry starts to trouble her again. She thinks, "Sure, *my* dad is an excellent driver, but what about all the other, bad drivers?" So she asks Mom again, "Are you sure Dad will be okay?" This time, Mom says, "Of course he will; it is a very short trip." The girl nods: that's also a good point, it's not a long drive at all.

But in a few minutes, the girl starts worrying again. After all, car accidents can happen at any time, can't they? It really doesn't matter how long the drive is. So she asks her Mom again, "Are you sure he's okay?" By now, Mom is getting a little irritated. "Yes, he's fine! Stop asking me this question and go do your homework."

Here's the problem. There's *nothing* that Mom can possibly say to make her daughter's worry disappear. Because the truth is, people sometimes get in car accidents. Is it likely that Dad will get in a crash on his 15-minute drive home from work? No—in fact it is highly unlikely. And even if he did, chances are that it would be a minor fender bender and nothing life-threatening. But nobody can promise with 100 percent certainty that a bad accident will definitely not happen.

Eventually, her dad will come home from work, and she will stop worrying about his safety, at least for tonight. Instead, she might start worrying about the possibility of a pop quiz at school the next day, or a burglar breaking into the house, or a terrorist attack,

EDUCATIONAL VIDEO

Scan this code for a video about stress and anxiety.

or . . . the possibilities are endless. And tomorrow, her dad has to make that 15-minute drive all over again.

Reassurance-seeking behaviors are a reaction to the uncertainty of life. We want authority figures—parents, teachers, and so on—to promise us that nothing bad will happen. But that's not a promise anyone can actually keep. We aren't fortune tellers, and we can't guarantee what will happen in the future.

The way to stop reassurance-seeking behaviors is not to finally "be reassured," because that will never happen. Instead, the anxious person needs to learn how to *live with* a certain level of uncertainty. For people with naturally anxious personalities, that can be tricky to learn.

THE SPIRAL

The human imagination is a wonderful thing. It has given us great books and movies, terrific music, and all kinds of fantastic art. Unfortunately, for people with anxiety problems, their imaginations can make daily life much more challenging than it needs to be. And our uncertain world provides an endless list of things to worry about.

Let's return to the example in the last section. When her mom got irritated, she told the girl to stop thinking about her dad's car and go do homework. So, the girl goes up to her room and tries to study for her history test. But the anxiety is still there,

If you feel like you are getting sucked into an anxiety spiral, checking in with a friend can help bring you back to reality.

and her worries make it impossible to focus on the American Revolution.

And then it gets worse. She thinks, "Not only is Dad probably in a car accident, but now Mom is mad at me, too." What if her mom gets so mad that she refuses to take the girl to gymnastics practice? The team has a big meet coming up! The girl is pretty sure she'll do badly anyway . . . but she'll definitely fall off the beam if her mom won't take her to practice! Then the whole school will see her fail and they'll all laugh at her, and she'll probably get kicked off the team. But, of course, the girl is definitely going to get kicked off the team if she fails this history test, which she can already tell she's going to because she can't concentrate. . . . By this point, the girl feels much, much worse than when she started.

This is sometimes called an *anxiety spiral.* One worry leads to the next, which leads to the next. And each worry is more dire than the one before, which makes the person that much more upset, which makes him or her worry even more, and so on.

The anxiety spiral can sometimes end in a panic attack, but more often it just results in misery and a terrible night's sleep. Fortunately, there are things you can do to try and stop the spiral before it gets out of control. That's what we'll cover in the next chapter.

RESEARCH PROJECT

The Anxiety Spiral Game (https:// cmhc.utexas.edu/ stressrecess/Level_ Two/anxiety_spiral. html) lets you explore what to say and what not to say in order to help your friend "Sally" find a way out of her anxiety spiral. Play the game, paying attention to the options offered. Why are some statements more helpful than others?

TEXT-DEPENDENT QUESTIONS

1. What are the physical signs of anxiety?

2. Does asking for reassurance work? Why or why not?

3. What is the anxiety spiral?

Talk to somebody you trust about what worries you.

CHAPTER FOUR

TAKING CHARGE OF ANXIETY

You know who doesn't have anxiety? Mr. Spock, the character on *Star Trek*. There are two main reasons why.

First, Spock is not from Earth; he is a Vulcan. Vulcans are famous for being completely logical. They base everything on facts, never on emotion. Most of what makes you anxious is your mind inventing things that haven't happened and might never happen. Spock doesn't have anxiety because he doesn't think about things that aren't real. So, when we're feeling worried, it can be helpful to think, "What would Mr. Spock do?"

But do you know the *other* reason he never has anxiety? Because he is a fictional character! All real humans have anxiety sometimes. So don't be too hard on yourself if you don't always feel quite as logical as him.

IMMINENT AND REMOTE

One thing Spock and his fellow logically minded people understand is the distinction between **imminent** and **remote** dangers. Imminent dangers

WORDS TO UNDERSTAND

adequate: sufficient amount; enough of something.

imminent: about to happen.

remote: very far away, either in time or space.

A possible bus accident falls under the category of "remote danger" because such accidents are extremely rare.

are probably worth our attention, while remote dangers may not be.

Let's say you're riding the bus to school and the driver suddenly slams on the brakes, sending your backpack flying onto the floor. In that moment, you are experiencing imminent danger: something happened and you could be injured. But if you worry about getting into an accident every time you get on the bus, you are worrying about a remote danger. Could it happen? Yes, maybe—bus accidents do happen occasionally. But is it likely to happen? No, it's not. Millions of kids take buses to and from school every day, in every city and town in the country, and there are rarely any problems.

The human imagination is a funny thing. Remote dangers can seem every bit as scary—sometimes even scarier!—than imminent ones. There's no shame in being afraid of remote dangers. The trick is to understand what your fear is about, so that you can manage it and not let it ruin your day.

SPIRAL DO'S AND DON'TS

Here's some advice for getting out of anxiety spirals.

Do: Be nice to yourself. A lot of people with anxiety get mad at themselves for feeling the way they do. People with anxiety tend to feel anxious about the fact that they feel anxious! But you are not a bad or weak person just because you have anxiety. Think of it this way: if your best friend was anxious about something, would you tell your friend that he or she is stupid for feeling that way? Of course not. Be as nice to yourself as you would be to a friend.

Don't: Try to "not think about it." Right now, please pause your reading for just a second and do the following:

1. Do not think about the elephant pictured on this page.
2. Do not think about that elephant, I said.
3. Seriously, cut it out. *Stop thinking about the elephant.*

How'd that work? Not well, right? Nope, because telling yourself not to think about something pretty much never works.

Do: Focus on the *facts* of the situation. What do you know for sure? In the last chapter, there was a story about a girl who is worried about her father's commute

Forcing yourself to stop thinking about your worries works about as well as forcing yourself to stop thinking about this elephant.

QUESTION YOURSELF

Anxiety involves your thoughts, and you can use your thoughts to combat it. When you start to feel anxious, try asking yourself the following questions. They can help you get some perspective on your situation.

- What is making me feel anxious?
- Is it something that's likely to happen?
- If it did happen, how bad would that actually be?
- Is the thing I'm worrying about really true, or is it just my perception?
- Is there anything I can do right now to affect what happens?

home from work. She pictures all sorts of terrible things that might happen. But what she should do is focus on facts. The girl only knows three things for sure: (1) her dad is on his way home from work, (2) it is a short trip from his job to home, and (3) it is a trip he has made hundreds of times before. That's it. Everything else is just "what ifs" that she is inventing. When you get anxious, try to refocus yourself on the facts of your situation. Is there an imminent danger or a remote one?

ANXIETY TOOLBOX

Here are some practical steps you can take to manage your anxiety:

- **Mind your fuel.** Make sure that you are eating right and getting enough sleep. This might seem like strange advice, since anxiety is something you feel, rather than a physical illness you "catch" like a cold. But emotions are not as separate from your body as you might think. After all, thoughts and feelings come from your brain. And your brain is an organ, just like your lungs are. If you breathe air that's filled with smoke, you are taking in a lot of junk that's going to make you cough. If you not sleeping enough or eating too much unhealthy food, you are also taking in junk that can make you feel worse. **Adequate** sleep and good nutrition are like fuel in a car; the better quality fuel you use, the better your machine will run.

- **Get moving!** Another way to make your "machine" work better is to use it more. Try to add some form of physical activity to your day. You don't have to join a team or be any kind of amazing athlete. You could take a walk, go for a swim, or even chase your little brother around the house.

- **Take it offline.** The Internet is an amazing technology that has completely changed the way we interact. And this is great, to a point. But it can also turn into a sort of echo chamber where people just make each other more and more upset. Make sure you get away from social media sometimes.

- **Establish a "worry time."** Sit down with an adult you trust and talk about what makes you anxious. Set a timer for a particular amount of time—some doctors say 10 minutes is

EDUCATIONAL VIDEO

Check out this video for more advice on coping with anxiety.

Physical activity is a great way to get your mind off your anxiety for a while.

good—and talk about whatever makes you fearful. There are no rules to this part of the exercise; you can talk about anything, from failing a test to surviving an alien invasion. The only rule is this: when the timer goes off, it is time to stop worrying about what *might* happen and go back to real life. The idea is to express what's on your mind (or "get it off your chest," as people sometimes say) and then make a conscious decision to move forward.

- **Write things down.** Another technique is to make a list of your anxieties. Some people find that putting "bad thoughts" down on paper makes those thoughts less scary. Once you have written your worries down, you can look at them more objectively, and you can think about how likely each fear actually is. Frequently, we worry about things that are very unlikely to happen.

Similarly, some therapists suggest having a "worry box." It could be an imaginary box, or you could even have an actual box where you write down what makes you anxious. Then you put the box away (or, if the box is imaginary, you envision yourself putting it way). Like "worry time," the idea of a box can help people acknowledge that their fears are real and then make a conscious decision to set them aside for a while.

- **Trick Your Anxiety.** There are a few parts to this final tip. First, don't try to talk yourself out of anxiety. Instead, accept that you feel anxious and remind yourself that it happens to everybody sometimes. Then remind yourself that anxiety involves worry about remote ideas, not concrete facts. In essence, anxiety is a trick your brain is playing on you. If you focus on the facts of your situation rather than on possibilities that may never happen, you can outwit your own brain and send your anxiety packing.

RESEARCH PROJECT

Research breathing skills and find out about how you can use breathing to ease your anxiety. You can find out about them at www. anxietycoach.com/ breathingexercise. html, or on similar websites. Practice the techniques, and write down how you feel before and after you try the skills.

TEXT-DEPENDENT QUESTIONS

1. What's the difference between imminent and remote dangers, and why does it matter?

2. What are some ways to stop the anxiety spiral?

3. What are three other things you can do to reduce anxiety?

FURTHER READING

Bourne, Edmund. *The Anxiety and Phobia Workbook.* 6th ed. Oakland, CA: New Harbinger, 2015.

Carbonell, David A. *The Worry Trick: How Your Brain Tricks You into Expecting the Worst and What You Can Do About It.* Oakland, CA: New Harbinger Publications, 2016.

Dwyer, Lucy. "When Anxiety Hits at School." *The Atlantic*, October 3, 2014. http://www.theatlantic.com/health/archive/2014/10/ when-anxiety-hits-at-school/380622/.

Poole, H. W. *Anxiety Disorders*. New Broomall, PA: Mason Crest, 2016.

Tartakovsky, Margarita. "9 Ways to Reduce Anxiety Right Here, Right Now." PsychCentral, 2016. http://psychcentral.com/ lib/9-ways-to-reduce-anxiety-right-here-right-now/.

West Virginia University Students' Center of Health. "CBT Strategies for Anxiety Relief." http://well.wvu.edu/articles/ cbt_strategies_for_anxiety_relief.

EDUCATIONAL VIDEOS

Chapter One: GoZen. "Fear vs. Anxiety." https://youtu.be/0v5E6syVppl.

Chapter Two: TeenMentalHealth.org. "Tom Has Separation Anxiety Disorder." https://youtu.be/jEkFp0Ux4OQ.

Chapter Three: TEDx Talks. "Be the Warrior, Not the Worrier." https://youtu.be/-FyVetL1MEw.

Chapter Four: Brian Johnson. "Conquering Anxiety 101." https://youtu.be/1fF0W_VhEcg.

SERIES GLOSSARY

adaptive: a helpful response to a particular situation.

bias: a feeling against a particular thing or idea.

biofeedback: monitoring of bodily functions with the goal of learning to control those functions.

cognitive: relating to the brain and thought.

comorbid: when one illness or disorder is present alongside another one.

context: the larger situation in which an event takes place.

diagnose: to identify an illness or disorder.

exposure: having contact with something.

extrovert: a person who enjoys being with others.

harassment: picking on another person frequently and deliberately.

hypnosis: creating a state of consciousness where someone is awake but highly open to suggestion.

inhibitions: feelings that restricts what we do or say.

introvert: a person who prefers being alone.

irrational: baseless; something that's not connected to reality.

melatonin: a substance that helps the body regulate sleep.

milestone: an event that marks a stage in development.

motivating: something that makes you want to work harder.

occasional: from time to time; not often.

panic attack: sudden episode of intense, overwhelming fear.

paralyzing: something that makes you unable to move (can refer to physical movement as well as emotions).

peers: people who are roughly the same age as you.

perception: what we see and believe to be true.

persistent: continuing for a noticeable period.

phobia: extreme fear of a particular thing.

preventive: keeping something from happening.

probability: the likelihood that a particular thing will happen.

psychological: having to do with the mind and thoughts.

rational: based on a calm understanding of facts, rather than emotion.

sedative: a type of drug that slows down bodily processes, making people feel relaxed or even sleepy.

self-conscious: overly aware of yourself, to the point that it makes you awkward.

serotonin: a chemical in the brain that is important in moods.

stereotype: an oversimplified idea about a type of person that may not be true for any given individual.

stigma: a sense of shame or disgrace associated with a particular state of being.

stimulant: a group of substances that speed up bodily processes.

subconscious: thoughts and feelings you have but may not be aware of.

syndrome: a condition.

treatable: describes a medical condition that can be healed.

upheaval: a period of great change or uncertainty.

INDEX

adaptive response 15, 17, 23

adrenaline 9, 12, 13, 29

advice on coping 39–43

amygdala 9, 12, 13

anxiety

    compared to fear 15–16

    definition of 16

    human body and 28–30

    problems with 27–28, 29–30

    spiral 33–35, 39–40

    tips about 40–43

    uncertainty and 33

brain 12–13, 15–16, 29, 41, 43

danger, remote vs. imminent 37–39, 40

dark, fear of 20, 23–24

doctors and dentists, fear of 24

dogs, fear of 15–16, 20, 23, 29–30

fear

    ancestors and 9–12, 23

    babies and 20–23

    common by age 20

    compared to anxiety 15–16

    definition of 16

    human body and 12–15, 29

    kids and 23–25

    of dark 20, 23–24

    of doctors and dentists 24

    of dogs 15–16, 20, 23, 29–30

    of strangers 20–21

    See also specific fears

fight-or-flight response 12, 14

insomnia 26, 27, 30

maladaptive response 15

object permanence 19, 22

peek-a-boo 22

probability 25

reassurance-seeking behavior 30–33

self-care 39, 40–41

separation anxiety 20, 21–23

strangers, fear of 20–21

uncertainty 33

"worry time" 41–42

ABOUT THE ADVISOR

Anne S. Walters is Clinical Associate Professor of Psychiatry and Human Behavior at the Alpert Medical School of Brown University. She is also Chief Psychologist for Bradley Hospital. She is actively involved in teaching activities within the Clinical Psychology Training Programs of the Alpert Medical School and serves as Child Track Seminar Co-Coordinator. Dr. Walters completed her undergraduate work at Duke University, graduate school at Georgia State University, internship at UTexas Health Science Center, and postdoctoral fellowship at Brown University.

ABOUT THE AUTHOR

H. W. Poole is a writer and editor of books for young people, including the sets, *Families Today* and *Mental Illnesses and Disorders: Awareness and Understanding* (Mason Crest). She created the *Horrors of History* series (Charlesbridge) and the *Ecosystems* series (Facts On File). She has also been responsible for many critically acclaimed reference books, including *Political Handbook of the World* (CQ Press) and the *Encyclopedia of Terrorism* (SAGE). She was coauthor and editor of *The History of the Internet* (ABC-CLIO), which won the 2000 American Library Association RUSA award.

PHOTO CREDITS

Cover (clockwise): Shutterstock/brusni4ka; iStock/Sadeugra; Shutterstock/oliveromg; iStock/KatarzynaBialasiewicz
iStock: 8 skynesher; 10 Gastuner19; 11 KatarzynaBialasiewicz ; 14 AdShooter; 16 jaminwell; 18 princessdlaf; 21 kali9; 22 luba; 24 XiXinXing; 26 Ljupco; 28 sharply_done; 31 fstop123; 34 Feverpitched; 36 digitalskillet; 38 kali9; 39 Andrey_Kuzmin; 42 monkeybusinessimages
Shutterstock: 13 Blamb